The
Great Glen

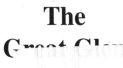

D0589591

A 73 Mile Walk from Fort William to Inverness
Along the Great Glen
Via the Caledonian Canal and Loch Ness

An Essential Guide to
Help You Complete
The Great Glen Way

Brian Smailes

You will never walk alone with these books published by
Challenge Publications

Top Ten series
THE YORKSHIRE DALES TOP TEN
ISBN 0-9526900-5-5

THE LAKELAND TOP TEN
ISBN 0-9526900-3-9

THE DERBYSHIRE TOP TEN
ISBN 1-903568-03-X

Other books
THE SCOTTISH COAST TO COAST WALK
ISBN 0-9526900-8-X

JOHN O'GROATS TO LANDS END
ISBN 0-9526900-4-7

THE COMPLETE ISLE OF WIGHT COASTAL FOOTPATH
ISBN 0-9526900-6-3

ISLE OF WIGHT, NORTH TO SOUTH – EAST TO WEST
ISBN1-903568-07-2

THE NATIONAL 3 PEAKS WALK
ISBN 0-9526900-7-1

THE YORKSHIRE 3 PEAKS WALK
ISBN 1-903568-01-3

THE LANCASHIRE TRAIL
ISBN 1-903568-10-2

THE 1066 COUNTRY WALK
ISBN 1-903568-00-5

MILLENNIUM CYCLE RIDES IN 1066 COUNTRY (EAST SUSSEX)
ISBN 1-903568-04-8

TOURIST GUIDE TO VARADERO, CUBA
ISBN 1-903568-08-0

ISBN 1-903568-13-7
FIRST PUBLISHED 2003
CHALLENGE PUBLICATIONS
7, EARLSMERE DRIVE, ARDSLEY, BARNSLEY. S71 5HH

Brian Smailes

Holds the record for the fastest 4 and 5 continuous crossings of the Lyke Wake Walk over the North York Moors. He completed the 210miles over rough terrain on 5 crossings in June 1995 taking 85hours and 50minutes.

Brian lectures on outdoor pursuit courses and between these travels extensively on walking expeditions and projects around Great Britain.

Long distance running and canoeing are other sports he enjoys, completing 25 marathons and canoeing the Caledonian Canal 3 times.

His most recent venture involved cycling from Lands End to John O`Groats in August 2001, a journey of over 900miles in 6days 13hours 18minutes. This involved carrying food, clothing and tent, and was completed without any support between both ends.

Having travelled extensively around Europe and the Caribbean, Brian is currently writing international travel guides to enable the holidaymaker to access the world with ease and enjoy it as much as he does.

ACKNOWLEDGEMENTS

In publishing this 1st edition of The Great Glen Way I must thank the following people for their help and contribution: -

Trevor Atkinson for photographs and support along the route.

Alastair MacLeod Route Manager of The Great Glen Way Ranger Service, for his help and advice.

ISBN 1-903568-13-7
First Published 2003
Published by: - Challenge Publications, 7 Earlsmere Drive, Barnsley, S71 5HH
Printed by: - Dearne Valley Printers Ltd. Tel: 01709 872188

CONTENTS

Useful information

PHOTOGRAPHS

Page

Drawings

FOREWORD

The Great Glen Way, a 73mile/117km walk through some of the most spectacular scenery in Scotland. This first edition of this book gives you the route in detail, facts, figures and necessary information to enable you to complete the walk in safety and to help you enjoy it, and the breathtaking views throughout it's length.

Starting near the shore of Loch Linnhe in Fort William and within sight of Britain's highest mountain Ben Nevis, the walk passes through Fort Augustus, Invermoriston and Drumnadrochit. Nearby stands Urquhart Castle, overlooking Loch Ness, and where visitors come to look for the monster of this deep Loch. The route of the Great Glen Way takes you high above Loch Ness where you too can look down over the Loch, not for monsters but to admire the views, the peaks and the glens that are part of this walk and part of Scotland.

After walking through woodland, by loch side, over mountains and on canal towpath you finally ascend to the terminus plinth at Inverness Castle *(Plate 12)* and probably a well-earned rest. Before leaving, take time to explore Inverness and sample all that this historic city has to offer. I hope you enjoy this remarkable walk as I did, and that when you finish, you have a sense of achievement and have been rewarded amply for your efforts in many ways.

I found that on this walk, although compass use was not necessary, it is still advisable to take one with you for emergency use.

Within this book The Great Glen Way is often referred to as G.G.W.

ACCESS TO FORT WILLIAM

Fort William is situated in the North West of Scotland at the start, or end of the Caledonian Canal and in the shadow of Britain's highest mountain, Ben Nevis. It is also the start or end of the Great Glen, which runs to Inverness and includes Loch Ness, also situated in the Great Glen.

By Road: -

From the west side of the UK - access to Scotland is by the M6 then A74M and M74, directly to Glasgow. Take the M8 approaching Glasgow and follow the A82 towards Dumbarton and Loch Lomond. Take the winding road heading north by the side of Loch Lomond then pass through Crianlarich and Tyndrum before taking the right fork towards Fort William. Pass through picturesque Glen Coe still on the A82, then cross the bridge at Ballachulish, approaching Loch Linnhe to Fort William.

From the east side of the UK - take the A69 to Corbridge from Newcastle, turning onto the A68 to Jedburgh then Edinburgh. At Edinburgh, take the M8 to Glasgow before following the A82 Dumbarton road to pass Loch Lomond, Crianlarich and Tyndrum. Continue on this road through Glen Coe to Fort William.

By Rail: -

Access to Fort William is available from all major cities of the UK. The railway station in Fort William is only 80m from the start of The Great Glen Way. The journey may involve changing trains at some point on your journey but ask when booking. Daily services are available from Inverness, Glasgow and Edinburgh to Fort William.

By Air: -

Flights from Gatwick and Luton to Inverness are available and to Glasgow from other airports in the UK. These are liable to change so contact the airports to obtain current flight details. A coach service is available from Glasgow and Inverness to Fort William.

See section on Useful Information for telephone numbers etc.

Distances to Fort William

from: -

	Miles		Miles
Inverness	70	Leeds	335
Glasgow	100	Liverpool	335
Edinburgh	145	Birmingham	409
Newcastle	239	London	522

THE GREAT GLEN

This stretches from Fort William to Inverness and through it runs the Caledonian Canal. Mountains on either side of the canal, tower high above the towns and villages situated in the Great Glen. Aonach Mor and Ben Nevis to the south west provide an impressive backdrop to Fort William and to the north east is Sron a' Choire Garbh and Ben Tee overlooking Loch Lochy.

The Great Glen is famous for the Loch Ness monster, said to live in Loch Ness, an ancient sea loch but now cut off directly from the sea and part of the Caledonian Canal.

Although the main A82 road runs through the Glen, the walking route of the Great Glen Way takes you at low level along by the canal, with high level sections which skirt the contours of the mountains, through forest and over fells, on paths and tracks, giving unparalleled views of the glen at every turn.

There are a number of interesting places situated throughout the glen like the flight of locks near the start of the walk, known as Neptune's Staircase, the commando memorial near Spean Bridge *(Plate 2),* the Clan Cameron Museum at Achnacarry near Clunes, the Well of Seven Heads near Loch Oich and Urquhart Castle overlooking Loch Ness.

No matter where you are in the Great Glen you can be sure of a warm welcome and a good holiday, though I cannot predict the weather!

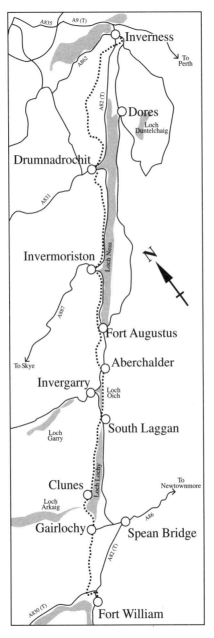

Plan of Route

FORT WILLIAM AREA

Fort William is the main town near the foothills of Ben Nevis. It also represents the start or end of the Caledonian Canal and the Great Glen Way, which connects with Inverness.

A tourist information centre in Fort William provides interesting displays of local attractions as well as general information about the area. The Glen Nevis Visitor Centre gives a more comprehensive guide to the Glen and the local area, also information, on Ben Nevis.

The road along Glen Nevis runs for approximately 7miles. You will find the visitor centre, the youth hostel and the Glen Nevis Caravan & Camping Park, which is an excellent site and the main one in the area for people accessing Ben Nevis or walking The Great Glen Way, along this road. The route to the summit of Ben Nevis starts from the visitor centre in Glen Nevis near the camping park.

There are mountains to climb, whisky distilleries to visit, cable cars and cruises to venture on. Local restaurants around Fort William offer good food. Loch Linnhe borders Fort William and there is fishing and sailing for those who enjoy alternative sports. Within the area there are many outdoor activity centres, which cover other water sports and land-based activities.

Many of the buildings are stone built and the town is clean and pleasant. The local people welcome visitors and there are numerous hostelries in which to sample local ale. There are a number of outdoor shops selling maps, compasses and most outdoor equipment should you need any last minute items.

Those walkers who have time to relax before walking The Great Glen Way will find the area around Fort William very pleasant and picturesque.

INVERNESS AREA

Inverness is situated on the east coast in the heart of the highlands. It is Britain's millennium city, exciting and scenic. Inverness is of course the end (can be the start) of The Great Glen Way, which finishes at Inverness Castle in the heart of the city *(Plate 12).*

Like Fort William, Inverness is the eastern gateway to the far highlands and islands, a bustling city of 65,000 people. The River Ness runs through the city to the Beauly Firth and the ancient battleground of Culloden where Bonnie Prince Charlie's troops were defeated in 1746 is only a short distance away.

There are a wealth of attractions in Inverness including the Aquadrome, Whin Park and Eden Court Theatre and the tropical delights of Bught Floral Hall.

Many of the buildings in Inverness are stone built, and the city centre combines the Victorian style market, the modern Eastgate Centre and the High Street. There are fine walks on the banks of the River Ness and on the towpaths of the Caledonian Canal, which was completed in 1822 and which links Inverness with the west coast

There are many hotels, guesthouses, B&Bs, and hostel accommodation, restaurants and cafés in Inverness and visitors are made welcome. The tourist information centre in the city centre are pleased to offer helpful advice about the area.

Inverness is regularly recognised in the Britain in Bloom and Beautiful Scotland awards. The quality of life research group recently ranked it fifth out of 189 towns and cities in Britain. Perhaps when you finish your walk you may have time to look around this historic city and sample all it has to offer.

QUESTIONS YOU MAY ASK

What time of year should I walk the G.G.W?

Obviously the best time to walk is in the summer months when it is supposed to be drier and warmer, but this is Scotland. It can be cold, rain and even snow in the summer months and equally you can have a nice calm, sunny day in winter. Generally though, the summer months are better but remember, if you walk in winter the days are shorter so leave enough time to reach your intended stop for the night.

In winter there are no midges to annoy you and there may be less frequent transport to take you from A to B
In summer you may find it hard to get booked in B&Bs on route unless you book early.

How long will the walk take?

There are a number of factors, which affect the daily distance you can travel, these are: -

Available Accommodation on route.
Weather Conditions
Fitness Level
Number of People Travelling in Your Group
Weight of Rucksack

How should I plan my daily mileage and stops?

Day			Miles	Km
1	**Fort William**	**to Gairlochy**	**10.5**	**16.8**
2	**Gairlochy**	**to Fort Augustus**	**22.5**	**36**
3	**Fort Augustus**	**to Invermoriston**	**8**	**12.8**
4	**Invermoriston**	**to Drumnadrochit**	**14**	**22.4**
5	**Drumnadrochit to Inverness**		**18**	**28.8**
			73	**116.8**

This suggested walk of five days would give you an easier first day, and a longer second day, although not too strenuous as a good proportion of it is on towpath or level ground. The third day would be shorter but there is more to see and do around Fort Augustus and it will probably be a welcome break to attend to feet or buy provisions for the next leg of the journey before walking the 8miles to Invermoriston.

The fourth day is more challenging with a stiff climb from Invermoriston, and of reasonable length to make some headway on your journey but not too long as to make you exhausted for the last day. Your final day will be the hardest with a stiff climb, which seems to go on and on. With the knowledge of what goes up must come down and the prospect of the finish in Inverness you will arrive at the finishing plinth exhausted but hopefully overwhelmed at what you have just achieved and experienced on route.

How can I avoid blisters?

Here is some simple tips that will help you avoid blisters but it is not guaranteed to work: -

Take plenty of socks and change them every 10miles, putting talc on feet to refresh them. You will feel a lot better. Ensure boots are a good fit, not too tight to cramp you feet but not too slack, otherwise feet move around and blisters form!

Do not wait until you have a blister before you do something about it. Put on some moleskin, adhesive plasters, second skin or other suitable dressing.

You can rub your feet with surgical spirit (available from chemist) for three weeks before you leave home to toughen them.

You could try a brand of socks called 1000-mile socks, which basically are two layers of sock that rub together instead of one layer rubbing against your skin and causing a blister. These are available from many outdoor shops.

Take a pair of trainers or walking shoes that you can change into on the flat towpath sections to give your feet a break from your boots. Boots should generally be worn on this walk for all sections apart from roads and towpaths.

Do I have to carry a rucksack?

You can have all your main equipment transported to your next stop but you should carry spare clothing, drinks, food and emergency items such as a whistle, torch and survival bag in a small day sack.

Are there shops on route to buy provisions, sweets/ drinks etc?

There are shops in Fort William, Fort Augustus, Invermoriston, Drumnadrochit and Inverness but nothing in between, although Great Glen Water Park just past North Laggan has a café/restaurant. You will need to take enough food and drinks to last the day or until you reach one of the places stated above. You may be able to get water from a house or lockkeeper on route but do not count on it.

What if I cannot complete the walk?

The main A82 road is not far away from the walking route for the majority of the walk, with villages and clusters of houses situated at regular intervals along the route. It is possible to get public transport to either end of the route and the places between. Buses tend to stop in the villages, but you need to check bus times.

Is the walk on towpath all the way, and flat?

Parts of the route are on towpath but as you get further into the walk there are more steep hilly sections. These are just past Invermoriston and especially on the last section just past Drumnadrochit. As these are high-level routes for several miles you need to be properly prepared with the right equipment and with food and drinks to give you energy on route.

Is the route safe to walk?

Yes, the route is safe as long as you keep to the paths and tracks, not venturing too near the edge of the canal or off the mountain track. Take care at all times while walking. It is good practice to inform someone of your intended route and stopping place, even completing a route card for yourself and giving a copy to someone who can monitor your progress.

PREPARATION

Before attempting this walk you need to prepare, not just by having the right equipment but researching the route and map before you travel and ensuring you are fit to walk the 73miles of this route, which can be demanding with both high and low level sections.

The best way to prepare physically for the walk is by walking various routes the weeks before you go or by generally keeping fit with running, swimming, cycling or other sport, which can give you the stamina and fitness needed to be able to complete this walk. Those who do some type of exercise in preparation, usually succeed, those who get in a car, drive from A to B and do no exercise do not!

Food
The food you consume while walking can affect your body heat and energy level. High-energy food such as bananas, rice, pasta, potato and wholemeal bread are all carbohydrate rich and of benefit. A high intake of these carbohydrates coupled with a balanced diet of protein, for building body and muscle strength, should give you the strength and energy to complete this walk.

Familiarisation
Study your map and familiarise yourself with the route and various landmarks, initially on the map, then if possible by visiting the area before you walk. Note where the telephone kiosks are for emergency, and where there is possible shelter i.e. villages etc in the event of severe inclement weather especially on the high level sections.

EQUIPMENT SELECTION

Carefully select both personal and safety equipment. Clothing should protect you from the elements as well as the changes in temperature that occur between the glen and the mountain track.

Boots

A good fitting pair of boots can make the difference between success or failure on any walk. Ankle protection is important especially where stones scattered on the track throughout large parts of the route and uneven ground can inflict damage very easily.

Most types of leather boots will need 'breaking-in' before use. Regular waxing will help keep the leather soft and supple. A sewn-in tongue will help prevent water and small stones getting into the boot. Before buying boots always try them on wearing the socks you will use with them. The boots should not be too tight as to cramp your toes likewise not too slack that your feet move around inside.

Socks

Some walkers prefer to wear 2 pairs of socks, others only one. Whatever your choice they should ideally be approximately 60% wool for good insulating property. Some socks have a thick base to help cushion the feet. You can usually buy short, medium and long depending on preference.

Trousers

Should be loose fitting and ideally made of cotton or a fleece type of material. Cotton trousers will be light to wear, keep you warm and most importantly will dry quickly when wet. Fleece trousers will generally keep you very warm. They are lightweight and can be waterproofed.

Jeans are not suitable for walking at all as they take a long time to dry when wet and become very heavy. They can also chafe the skin, draw the body heat and their insulating property is very low.

Hat

Much of the body's heat is lost through the head, so some protection is strongly advised. Woolly hats were the old favourite, however fleece ones are becoming more popular.

Jacket

Your jacket is one of the most important items as it will insulate your main body and help keep a constant body temperature. Fleece jackets are popular, as are breathable fabric jackets. A hood attached with a drawstring will give good protection around the head and full length two-way zips help to regulate body heat as well as allowing for ease in putting on/taking off in a harsh environment. These types of jackets are washable and can be waterproofed to withstand the elements.

Many people buy breathable jackets, which are waterproof and windproof. When the outside becomes wet it ceases to be breathable and you may get condensation building up inside. These jackets are only breathable when dry, so make your choice carefully as they are expensive. Whichever jacket you are buying, ensure it is waterproof and not just shower proof.

Features to look for on waterproof jackets are: -
• Full length two-way zip to help to regulate body heat and with putting on/taking off. It should also have a flap over it.
• Side pockets also with a flap over to stop water entering.
• Draw string on the fitted hood.
• Elasticated or adjustable cuffs to stop wind flow through the jacket at times of high wind or when cold.

When buying your jacket make allowance for the other items of clothing you would normally wear underneath and indeed extra items for cold weather.

Trousers

Waterproof/breathable trousers should have an elasticated waist and/or drawstring. Zips on the lower legs are very beneficial as these enable you to put them on/take off without taking your boots off.

Finally all seams on jackets and trousers should be taped to ensure no water passes through. A little candle wax rubbed on the zips will help to keep them running smoothly and keep water out.

Do not wear water/windproofs that are not breathable any longer than necessary as quite often condensation builds up inside. Try to keep the jacket ventilated as much as possible to reduce the condensation.

Gaiters

Help to protect the lower leg from the wet or abrasive rock. When walking the route described, I feel there is not a great need to wear them. Gaiters should be waterproof and ideally breathable.

Gloves

Pair of fleece, woollen gloves or mittens are strongly recommended in times of adverse weather. You will find that 5-finger gloves, as opposed to mittens, are probably better, especially in strong wind when handling map or adjusting compass.

Rucksack

This should be large enough to hold all your personal and safety equipment described. A rucksack should ideally have wide padded shoulder straps and a waist belt to stop it moving around. It is advisable to put a liner inside to keep your clothes and other items dry in very wet conditions. External zipped pockets in which to put small or frequently needed items i.e. water bottle, map, food etc are very useful.

In summarising personal clothing and its effectiveness, the following points need to be remembered. Clothing should be built up in layers where warm air can be trapped between each one. Three thin tops are more effective than one thick one. If you are hot you can easily take a layer off.

Emergency Equipment

The following items may never be used but should always be carried in your rucksack. This includes spare clothing e.g. sweater, socks etc.

Torch

Each person should carry one; take spare batteries and a bulb. Check it works before each mountain.

Pencil & Notebook

It may be necessary to take notes on route, and especially in an emergency when positions, names, injuries etc. can be written and passed on to emergency services.

Whistle

Each person should carry a plastic whistle and they should be familiar with the 'S.O.S.' signal to alert others in times of emergency.

Survival Bag

Usually made of heavy-duty polythene and designed for a walker to get inside to protect them from the harsh environment and to preserve their body heat. It is a piece of essential equipment, which each person should carry.

First Aid Kit

Essential for all walkers, (see First Aid Section).

Map/Compass

May not be used on this walk, but recommended.

EQUIPMENT CHECKLIST

Tick

- Boots
- Socks
- Torch/Spare Bulb & Batteries
- Rucksack
- Whistle
- Hat
- Gloves
- Spare Clothing/Socks etc.
- First Aid Kit
- Maps/Compass
- Insect Repellent
- Sunscreen
- Toiletries
- Pencil/Notebook
- Waterproof/Windproofs
- Gaiters
- Water Bottle
- Survival Bag

If Camping
- Sleeping Bag
- Tent
- Stove/Fuel
- Food/Drinks
- Sleep Mat
- Tin Opener
- Cup/plate/cutlery
- Matches
- Pans

THE BODY

RUCKSACK
Containing food, drinks,
first aid, and clothing,
map and compass.

THE HEAD
Should be kept warm,
more heat is lost
from the head
than anywhere else.

THE BODY
Should be kept
warm.
Build clothes up
in layers with
wind/waterproofs
on top.

HANDS
Should be kept
warm
with gloves.

MAIN BODY CORE
Temperature must
be maintained.

LEGS
It is important not to
wear jeans

ANKLES
Should be protected
by wearing boots.
These will help stop
you going over on
your ankle and
strengthen it.

FEET
Should be kept well
cushioned and dry if possible.
Good fitting boots will help
prevent blisters

FIRST AID

Knowledge of basic first aid would be helpful on any walk. In any accident or emergency situation, reassuring the casualty and comforting them is very important, do not move the casualty if the accident is of a possible serious nature e.g. a back or head injury. Ensure the casualty is warm then send for help. Someone should stay with the injured person. If the injury is not of a serious nature the injured person should, if and when possible, be removed from danger.

Where there is the possibility of shock or delayed shock, reassurance and company is vital. It is a fact that the majority of accidents happen on the return or second half of the journey. This is probably due to fatigue, cold, tiredness or complacency.

Common Types of Injuries

Cuts and grazes	*Broken Arms/Legs*	*Cracked Ribs*
Blisters	*Hypothermia*	*Head Injuries*
Sprained Ankle/Wrist		*Gashed Shins*

All the above, however minor, can prove fatal with the casualty going into shock, especially in an exposed area or in times of panic, fog or adverse conditions, coupled with the injury.

In the event of an accident, 2 people should go for help; this should be the fittest person and best navigator. They should take their own personal safety equipment with them. Other people should stay with the injured person to help and reassure them.

Individual First Aid Kit

Adhesive Dressing	*Waterproof Container*	*Scissors*
Triangular Bandage	*Sterile Dressing*	*Micropore*
Bandage	*Crepe Bandage*	*Sun Cream*
Safety Pins	*Gauze/Lint*	*Insect Repellent*

HYPOTHERMIA

Hypothermia is caused when the body core temperature falls below 35°C. If a walker is not properly prepared for the conditions or the equipment/clothing is not satisfactory then a combination of the cold, wet, exhaustion and the wind chill factor can give a walker hypothermia.

The Signs and Symptoms in Descending Order: -

Shivering
Cold, pale and dry skin
Low body temperature
Irrational behaviour
A gradual slip into unconsciousness
Pulse and respiratory rate slow
Difficulty in detecting breathing and pulse when unconscious
Death

Ways of Preventing Hypothermia

1. Build up body clothing in thin layers, adding on or taking off as necessary.
2. Have suitable wind/waterproofs with you.
3. Take some food/hot drink or boiled sweets, which produce energy and heat during digestion.
4. Wear a balaclava/woolly hat to insulate the head, and some gloves.
5. Shelter out of the wind.
6. Take a survival bag and if conditions dictate, use it.

The temperature difference between the glen and the high ground can be several degrees. If the injured walker is able to move safely, descending to lower ground is usually the best solution.

When conditions do not permit movement and if you are in a sheltered area, stay where you are until such time as conditions improve. It may be at this time that you put on extra clothing and use survival bags.

Treatment for Hypothermia

1. Provide extra clothing and shelter from the elements.
2. Bodily warmth of others helps in a gradual warming.
3. If well enough come down into a warmer sheltered area.
4. Give hot drinks if conscious.
5. Give chocolate or sweets if the patient can still take food.
6. The casualty should be placed so that the head is slightly lower than the body.

DO NOT *rub the skin or use a hot water bottle as this can cause a surge of blood from the central body core to the surface, this could prove fatal.*

Alcohol should not be consumed on any walk and should not be given to anyone who has hypothermia. The body temperature will be lowered as well as giving a false sense of security.

THE COUNTRY CODE

The countryside is a place where many people like to escape to and enjoy at various times. To do this we need to look after it when we use it and to preserve it for future generations.

The following is a simple list of do's and don'ts to help everyone enjoy the countryside.

Do
- Guard against all risk of fire
- Fasten all gates
- Keep dogs under close control
- Use gates and stiles to cross walls and fences
- Protect wildlife, trees and plants
- Take litter home
- Leave nothing but footprints, take nothing but photographs
- Be conscious at all times of erosion of footpaths

Don't
- Play radios etc. or create unnecessary noise
- Take mountain bikes on walkways
- Touch machinery, livestock or crops

SUPPORT TEAM

There may be some people who have support and wish to perhaps stay at one location e.g. on the camping site in Glen Nevis and be supported on route with carrying of equipment and organised food stops on route, returning to Fort William after a days hard walking to start the following day where they left off the previous day.

I have attempted to show below, possible locations where a support vehicle could meet walkers on route for those who prefer this method.

Fort William – The main car park situated across from the roundabout near the start of the walk.

Banavie – Side of Neptune's Staircase at the top.

Gairlochy – Parking near the bridge over the lock.

Clunes – Just past the Clan Cameron Museum beside the forest.

Laggan Locks – Parking in a car park beside South Laggan Lock.

Aberchalder – Car park near the bridge.

Fort Augustus – Large car park in the centre next to the T.I.C.

Invermoriston – Car park just past the bridge on the right side when entering Invermoriston.

Balbeg – Small car park at side of single-track road.

Drumnadrochit – Large car park beside the T.I.C. on the route.

Ladycairn to Blackfold – Various pull-ins on route, short stops only.

Inverness – Parking near the Cathedral and in side streets (charge).

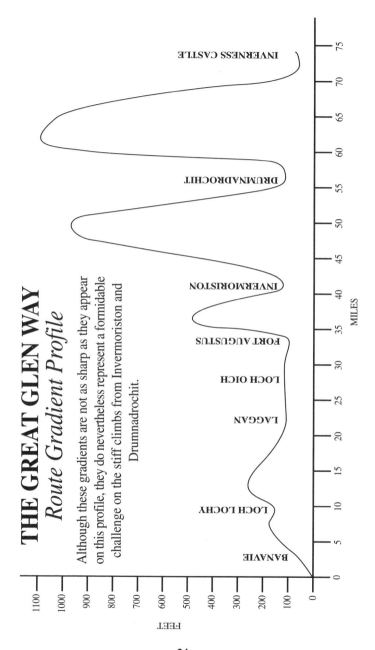

THE GREAT GLEN WAY
Route Gradient Profile

Although these gradients are not as sharp as they appear on this profile, they do nevertheless represent a formidable challenge on the stiff climbs from Invermoriston and Drumnadrochit.

INVERNESS CASTLE

DRUMNADROCHIT

INVERMORISTON

FORT AUGUSTUS

LOCH OICH

LAGGAN

LOCH LOCHY

BANAVIE

FEET

1100
1000
900
800
700
600
500
400
300
200
100
0

MILES

0 5 10 15 20 25 30 35 40 45 50 55 60 65 70 75

24

THE ROUTE IN DETAIL

The walking route of The Great Glen Way is also the cycling route for much of the distance, but in a number of places it splits into two separate routes. Ensure you take the walking route in these parts. Where the cycling route splits, it usually has a cycle sign or written sign indicating the two separate routes. The walking route is marked throughout with a white thistle, *(shown on plates 4 & 11).*

(See Map No.1)

Leaving the starting plinth *(Plate 1)* in Fort William near the roundabout G.R.105743, walk to the smaller round-about near the entrance to Safeway supermarket. Cross to the far side onto a footpath/cycle way alongside a pub, then continue along the rear of the Travel Inn. Keep on the footpath/cycle way, following it through a cluster of houses, over a bridge then left on a stony path taking you alongside the river.

Cross two wooden bridges in succession, still on the narrow stony path. View Ben Nevis off to your right as you join the unclassified public road. You then cross a long wooden bridge called The Soldiers Bridge, spanning the River Lochy.

Emerging onto a road, turn left to go through the village of Caol. Follow the footpath past Lochan Cottage Guest House. Just past the sign for St. Johns Roman Catholic Church, turn left, following the G.G.W. sign clockwise round the outskirts of the housing estate and along Erracht Drive, alongside the sea loch.

Passing a post office and small supermarket, continue skirting the sea loch. You pass Caol community centre then bear left approaching a football pitch, onto a narrow path close by the sea loch. Pass the football pitch and go through a small wooden gate bearing right on a stony footpath towards the Caledonian Canal. As you approach the canal, turn right onto the canal towpath, before going through a large wooden gate.

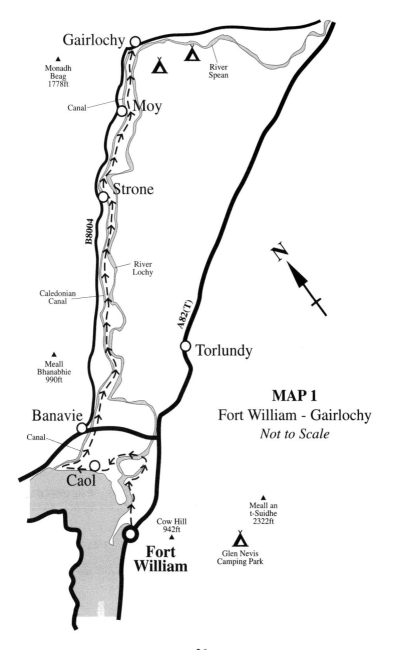

Gairlochy

Monadh
Beag
1778ft

River
Spean

Canal

Moy

Strone

B8004

River
Lochy

Caledonian
Canal

A82(T)

Meall
Bhanabhie
990ft

Torlundy

N

Banavie

Canal

MAP 1
Fort William - Gairlochy
Not to Scale

Caol

Cow Hill
942ft

Meall an
t-Suidhe
2322ft

Fort
William

Glen Nevis
Camping Park

Plate 1
The starting plinth in Fort William
with Ben Nevis in the background

UNITED · WE · CONQUER

Plate 2
The Commando Memorial at Spean Bridge

Keep on the towpath with the canal to your left until you reach the railway line near Neptune's Staircase. Cross the railway at the level crossing gates with care then cross the main A830 road. Ascend the gravel towpath/track on the right of the flight of locks. Continue on the towpath, passing through several gates to Moy Bridge, which is attractive, with picnic table nearby. Continue on the towpath to Gairlochy Bridge and the lock there.

(See Map No.2)

Look for the white thistle sign then cross the bridge over the canal, taking the second right following the G.G.W. signs. Now ascend a steep narrow metalled road, and as it levels out higher up, look for a G.G.W. marker post on your right to take you on a short steep descent to the side of Loch Lochy. Walk on the stony path alongside the loch, passing over several small footbridges spanning the burns.

Eventually the path ascends to return to the road where you turn right towards Clunes. You pass the entrance to the Clan Cameron Museum then at a bend in the road you turn right off the metalled road onto a wide track taking you through the forest towards the loch.

Continue on the undulating track close to the loch, passing over a cattle grid and through a gate in the deer fence. Stay on this track then as you reach the far end of the loch you will have a good view of South Laggan Locks ahead *(Plate 3)* to the right. Take a right fork as you approach the lock to take you past some chalets to the lock.

Cross the lock *(Plate 3)* looking for a small waymarker and finger post on your left at the far side, to take you onto a grass track close by the canal. After walking on the towpath for a short distance, you go onto a narrow wooded path near the canal, crossing a small footbridge before reaching the A82 road.

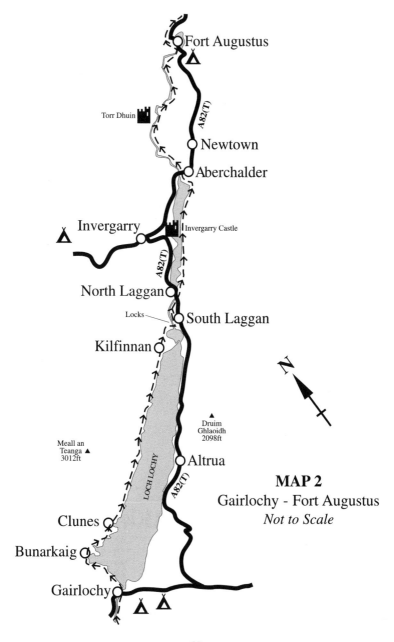

Fort Augustus

Torr Dhuin

A82(T)

Newtown

Aberchalder

Invergarry

Invergarry Castle

A82(T)

North Laggan

Locks

South Laggan

Kilfinnan

Druim
Ghlaoidh
2098ft

Meall an
Teanga ▲
3012ft

Altrua

A82(T)

LOCH LOCHY

MAP 2
Gairlochy - Fort Augustus
Not to Scale

Clunes

Bunarkaig

Gairlochy

N

Plate 3
South Laggan Locks where the G.G.W. crosses the lock.

Plate 4
Looking back up the flight of locks at Fort Augustus.
Note:- The G.G.W. sign and symbol.

Cross this busy road with care into the entrance of the Great Glen Water Park, following the marker posts past the chalets then onto a forest track nearby Loch Oich. Walk through a high kissing gate then over a long metal bridge spanning the river. Pass through another high kissing gate following the path round by the loch, then over steps before reaching Abercalder Bridge.

Cross the busy A82 with care by the bridge control room and walk down the right side of the canal on the towpath to the lock. Walk across the lock gates by the lockkeeper's cottage, following the G.G.W. arrows then walk on the towpath with the canal on your right. Continue on the towpath, passing Kytra Lock and eventually arriving in Fort Augustus. (The B&Bs are on both sides of the flight of locks *(Plate 4)* as you enter Fort Augustus).

(See Map No.3)

Descending to the main road at the foot of the locks *(Plate 5)* turn left, taking you past the Shell garage, T.I.C. and the main car park. While on the footpath, as you reach the far corner of the car park on the A82, look for a metal barrier at the side of the road then turn left at the waymarker post onto a tarmac path ascending a short distance to a minor road.

Turn left at the road, following it round then after descending a hill you come to a small stone bridge. Turn left just before it, following the marker post onto a narrow path by a stream, which soon ascends steeply through the forest. Look for the small marker posts in this demanding section. Stay on the path and track until eventually you come to a steep descent, turning right to pass two dwellings and emerging on the main A82 road at Invermoriston.

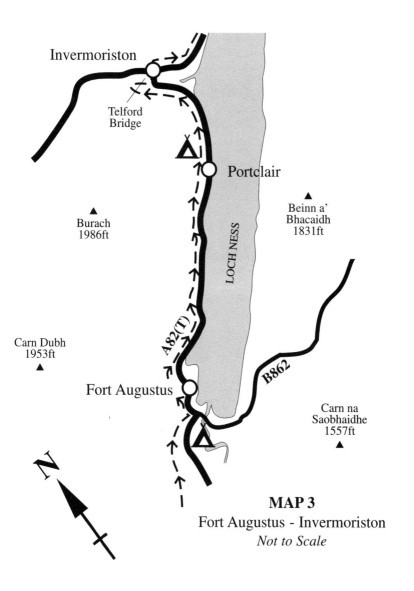

Invermoriston

Telford
Bridge

Burach
1986ft

Portclair

Beinn a'
Bhacaidh
1831ft

LOCH NESS

Carn Dubh
1953ft

A82(T)

Fort Augustus

B862

Carn na
Saobhaidhe
1557ft

N

MAP 3
Fort Augustus - Invermoriston
Not to Scale

Plate 5
Descending the locks at Fort Augustus with
Loch Ness beyond.

Plate 6
Thomas Telfords Old Bridge, Invermoriston.

Plate 7
The forest track between Invermoriston and Drumnadrochit
with Loch Ness in the background below.

Plate 8
Loch Ness with Urquhart Castle on the point in the centre

(See Map No. 4)

Turn left to cross the main bridge passing Telfords old bridge nearby *(Plate 6)*. Walk to the right hand bend in the road (two B&Bs opposite). Turn left at the bend then right on a long steep climb on a metalled road. Nearing the top, cross a small wooden bridge, turning immediately right onto a wide track, which becomes a narrow winding path leading towards Drumnadrochit.

Continue through the forest *(Plate 7)* on the undulating but generally ascending path, passing a sign for the nearby youth hostel in the forest. The track bears left just past the Y.H. sign, ascending again as you follow the G.G.W. markers, eventually descending a stony track to the main A82 road into Drumnadrochit.

(See Map No. 5)

Turn left following the main A82 road through the village (B&Bs on right side). Continue on the road until you reach Tychat, and a house on its own on the left side called Temple House. Look for a G.G.W. marker post beside the entrance and walk on a path round the perimeter of the house.

The first half of this final section is the most demanding of the walk. Your path leaves the side of the house and runs nearby the road for a short distance before ascending steeply on a forest section of stony path and track *(Plate 8)*. Eventually you emerge near the top of the mountain, with spectacular views of Loch Ness between the trees.

You emerge on a wide, recently made stony forest road, which you stay on, veering away from the loch. The road ascends steeply then eventually descends to a building in the forest. Look for the waymarker then turn right onto a single-track road at Achpopuli. Stay on this to a junction then go straight across through a kissing gate onto a path you can see over the fence.

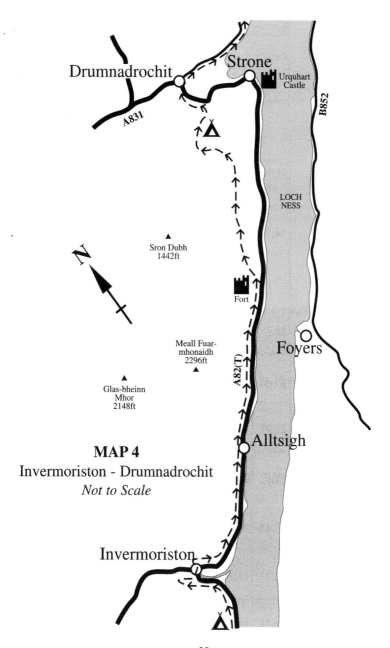

Drumnadrochit

Strone

Urquhart
Castle

A831

B852

LOCH
NESS

N

Sron Dubh
1442ft

Fort

Meall Fuar-
mhonaidh
2296ft

Foyers

A82(T)

Glas-bheinn
Mhor
2148ft

Alltsigh

MAP 4
Invermoriston - Drumnadrochit
Not to Scale

Invermoriston

Plate 9
The forest track just after turning off the road at Blackfold.

Plate 10
View of Inverness in the distance with the Beauly Firth
beyond the trees on the left.

Plate 11
The suspension bridge which you cross to Ness Islands.

Plate 12
The finishing plinth at Inverness Castle.

Stay on this gravel path winding past houses and up to a forest. Continue to a kissing gate at a single-track road where a G.G.W. fingerpost points left. Turn left here on the metalled road, a sign points to Caiplich. Continue on the road for 4.2miles/7km to a white house on your right, just before reaching a forest. Look for a fingerpost on your right, turning left then right, through a kissing gate onto a good path *(Plate 9)* generally descending through the forest towards Inverness.

Soon after entering the forest you have your first views of Beauly Firth *(Plate 10)*. You pass through another kissing gate near the far side of the forest then soon after turn right, following the G.G.W. marker to pass by an electricity pylon. Follow the short winding track to a small reservoir, go through a kissing gate onto a good small stone path, soon to descend steeply to another kissing gate.

Turn left to emerge at a hospital, follow the G.G.W. signs left, walking to the entrance at the main road. Look for the waymarker there pointing right, turn right for a short distance to the bend in the road then continue ahead, descending a narrow grass path directly into the glen towards Inverness.

The road passes behind a small housing estate then between it. Look for waymarkers as you descend to Torvean golf course. Follow the path through the course to emerge on the canal towpath. Turn right to Tomnahurich Bridge over the canal, cross then turn right along Bught Road, passing the leisure centre and follow the road anti-clockwise round a grassed area.

Keep on the path by the river to a metal footbridge, *(Plate 11)*, where you cross to Ness Islands. Follow the path to cross onto the right bank then turn left to walk on the path by the river. Nearing the castle look for an opening on your right, between the B&Bs and hotels, where a waymark sign points right along a narrow opening up some steps to a road.

Turn left on the road, walking the short distance to the castle and the plinth *(Plate 12)* that marks the finish of the Great Glen Way. Congratulations!

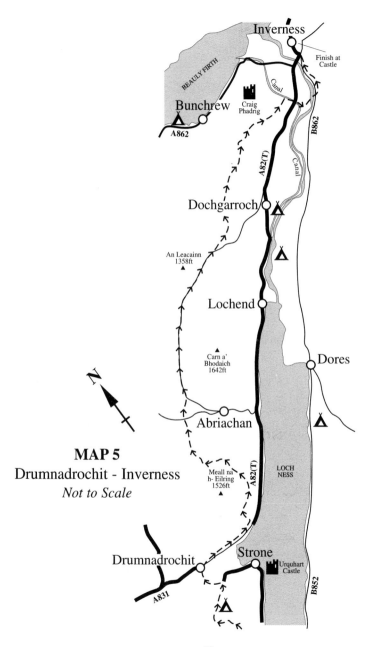

Inverness

Finish at
Castle

BEAULY FIRTH

Canal

Bunchrew

Craig
Phadrig

A862

A82(T)

Canal

B862

Dochgarroch

An Leacainn
1358ft

Lochend

Carn a'
Bhodaich
1642ft

Dores

N

Abriachan

MAP 5
Drumnadrochit - Inverness
Not to Scale

Meall na
h- Eilring
1526ft

A82(T)

LOCH
NESS

Strone

Drumnadrochit

Urquhart
Castle

A831

B852

42

PLACES OF INTEREST ON ROUTE

While in and around the Great Glen, you may wish to visit some of the attractions which are shown below, for a more comprehensive list or for more information contact the T.I.C. In practice you will probably not want to venture off-route once you have commenced the walk, so the list shown is not too long.

Fort William –
- Ben Nevis – The highest mountain in the UK and accessed from Glen Nevis via the mountain path from the Visitor Centre. Ensure you are properly prepared before you attempt it. Tel. 01397 705922 Easter – Oct. (Visitor Centre).
- Nevis Range – Take a trip in Scotland's only gondolas on the mountain of Aonach Mor situated at Torlundy near Fort William. Tel. 01397 705825
- Treasures of the Earth - Crystal and gemstone exhibition at Corpach, Fort William. Tel. 01397 772283
- Ben Nevis Distillery – See how the famous malts are made. Lochy Bridge, Fort William. Tel. 01397 702476
- Old Fort William – Look for parts of the original fort near the starting plinth *(Plate 1)* on the banks of Loch Linnhe in Fort William.

Spean Bridge –
- Commando Memorial situated at the side of the A82/B8004 just outside Spean Bridge *(Plate 2)*.

Achnacarry near Clunes –
- Clan Cameron Museum – Explore the clans history and its Jacobite links. Situated on route. Tel. 01397 712480

North Laggan –
- Well of the Seven Heads - between North Laggan and Invergarry. Built in 1812, this monument marks a clan massacre that took place in 1663.

Invermoriston –
- The old stone bridge - built by Thomas Telford around 1810 and eventually replaced in 1954. You pass it on route as you enter Invermoriston, *(Plate 6)*.

Drumnadrochit –

- Urquhart Castle - commands splendid views over Loch Ness *(Plate 8)*. Visitors come to look for the Loch Ness Monster from here.
The castle is 1mile from the route as you reach Drumnadrochit. Tel. 01456 450551

Inverness –

- Inverness Castle - built on the site of another former castle. Its use has been varied but it still stands prominent, overlooking the City. The plinth at the end of The Great Glen Way is situated outside the castle, *(Plate 12)*.
- Culloden Moor Visitors Centre - although situated 5miles outside Inverness, the battleground of Culloden is worth a visit. The place where the Jacobites were defeated in 1746 and from where Bonnie Prince Charlie fled is an eerie sight as you walk around the various encampments there. Tel. 01463 790607

POST WALK

On completing your expedition of The Great Glen Way, you may like a souvenir to mark your achievement. The author has produced a beautiful certificate to mark your achievement; priced at £1.00 for 2003/4 and sent post-free. Other items may be produced but a list will be sent either with order or on receipt of a S.A.E. Please send cheque with order payable to Brian Smailes: -

Challenge Publications
7, Earlsmere Drive,
Ardsley,
Barnsley
S.Yorks
S71 5HH

Visit our website at: -
www.chall-pub.fsnet.co.uk
E-mail – challengepublications@yahoo.co.uk

USEFUL INFORMATION

Recommended Maps
Ordnance Survey Explorer Maps 1:25 000 Scale
No.392 – Ben Nevis & Fort William
No.400 – Loch Lochy & Glen Roy
No.416 – Inverness, Loch Ness & Culloden
OR
Harvey's Maps 1:25 000 Scale
The Great Glen Way

Campsites on Route

There are no camping sites directly on the G.G.W. therefore you need to walk to a site, off the route. Wild Camping is not allowed on the G.G.W. Most sites are open Easter to October.
Fort William
Glen Nevis Caravan & Camping Park, Glen Nevis, Fort William. Tel: 01397 702191 An excellent site of the highest standard situated in Glen Nevis at the foothills of Ben Nevis and 2miles/3.3km from the start of the G.G.W.
Gairlochy
Gairlochy Holiday Park, Spean Bridge.
Tel. 01397 712711. (Between Canal & Commando Memorial).
Fort Augustus
Fort William Road. Tel. 01320 366618.
(1mile S.W. of the centre).
Invermoriston
Loch Ness Caravan & Camping Park. Tel. 01320 351207.
(On A82, 1mile S.W. of Invermoriston).
Drumnadrochit
Borlum Farm. Tel. 01456 450220
Inverness
Bught Caravan & Camping Site, The Bught.
Tel. 01463 236920. (Near the sports centre).

B&B Selection on Route

The following list of B&Bs has been chosen for reasonable prices, comfort and close proximity to the walking route. Most are directly on the route or as near as possible. They are not arranged in any order of priority other than route order so please choose at random. You are advised to book in advance especially during main holiday times. Some B&B's will cook evening meals so please ask when booking.

Aberchalder Baggage Transfer Service are able to transfer your baggage between all points on route, contact Jenny Keane, Tel: 01809 501411

Fort William

Mrs. J Orr, 'Taradale', Fassifern Road, Fort William. PH33 6BE
Tel: 01397 705704

Wilma & Jim McCourt, 6 Caberfeidh, Fassifern Road, Fort William. PH33 6BE Tel: 01397 703756
e-mail: caberfeidh6@btopenworld.com

Derek Walker, Constantia House, Fassifern Road, Fort William. PH33 6BD Tel: 01397 702893

Mrs. Wynne, St. Andrews House, Fassifern Road, Fort William. PH33 6BD Tel: 01397 703038
www.fortwilliam-accommodation.co.uk

The above are approx. 3-4 minutes walk to the start of the G.G.W.

Gairlochy

Dreamweavers, Earendil, Mucomir, by Spean Bridge PH34 4EQ Tel: 01397 712548 e-mail helen@dreamweavers.co.uk
www.fort-william.net/dreamweavers

The above is approx. 0.9 mile from the lock at Gairlochy but at the time of writing is the nearest to the route.

South Laggan

Mr.& Mrs Shearer, Forest Lodge Guest House, South Laggan.
PH34 4EA Tel: 01809 501219 Fax: 01809 501476
www.flgh.co.uk   e-mail: info@flgh.co.uk

The above is within sight of Laggan Locks on the A82

Fort Augustus

Mrs. Doreen Burridge, 'Balgonie', Canalside, Fort Augustus.
PH32 4BA Tel/Fax. 01320 366419 Mobile. 0775 4781282

Sue Callcutt, Tigh na Mairi, Canalside, Fort Augustus.
PH32 4BA Tel/Fax: 01320 366766 Mobile: 07714 337089
e-mail: suecallcutt@talk21.com

Kevin & Trudy Hodson, Caledonian House, Station Road, Fort
Augustus. PH32 4AY Tel: 01320 366236 Mobile: 0797 4522597
e-mail: cal@ipw.com   www.ipw.com/cal

The above are on route as you walk near the flight of locks
entering Fort Augustus.

Invermoriston

Mr & Mrs. S. Maclellan, Bracarina House, Invermoriston.
IV63 7YA Tel: 01320 351279 e-mail Sheila@maclellans.net
www.maclellans.net

Mrs I Greig, Georgeston, Invermoriston. Tel: 01320 351264
www.nessaccom.co.ukgeorgeston

The above are situated diagonally opposite the corner shop at
the road bend in Invermoriston.

Drumnadrochit

Rosalyn Luffman, The Green, Drumnadrochit. IV63 6TX
Tel/Fax: 01456 450865

Juliet Wynne, The Glen Bed & Breakfast, The Village Green, Drumnadrochit. IV63 6TX Tel: 01456 450279
Mobile 07831 372229 e-mail: bwynne@madasafish.com

The above are on route as you walk through Drumnadrochit.

Inverness
Jean & Tony Gatcombe, Ardmuir House, 16 Ness Bank, Inverness. IV2 4SF Tel/Fax: 01463 231151
e-mail: hotel@ardmuir.com
www.ardmuir.com

Chrysanne & Jack Bosworth, Silverwells, 28 Ness Bank, Inverness. IV2 4SF Tel: 01463 232113 (non-smoking)
e-mail: silver.wells@virgin.net

MacRae Guest House, 24 Ness Bank, Inverness. IV2 4SF Tel/Fax: 01463 243658   e-mail: joycemacrae@hotmail.com (non-smoking).

Felstead Guest House ★★★★, 18 Ness Bank, Inverness. IV2 4SF
Tel: 01463 231634   E-mail: felsteadgh@aol.com
http://www.jafsoft.com/felstead/felstead.html

The above are on route and approx. 3 minutes from the end of the walk at Inverness Castle.

Youth Hostels

There are four youth hostels along the G.G.W. these are: -
Fort William, Glen Nevis YH, Glen Nevis, Fort William.
Tel: 01397 702336

Loch Lochy, South Laggan, Spean Bridge, PH34 4EA
Tel: 01809 501239

Loch Ness (Alltsigh) Glenmoriston. IV3 6YD Tel:01320 351274
Access is on route after leaving Invermoriston, high on the forest track.

Inverness Victoria Drive, Inverness. IV2 3QB Tel: 01463 231771
Everyone is allowed to stay and use the facilities, member or not.

Central Booking for all YH Tel 0870 1553255

Information Centres in the Area

Glen Nevis Visitor Centre,
Glen Nevis. Tel 01397 705922 Open Apr – Oct

T.I.C. Fort William,
Cameron Square.   Tel 01397 703781

T.I.C. Fort Augustus,
The Car Park. Tel 01320 366367 Open Apr. - Oct.

T.I.C. Drumnadrochit
The Car Park. 01456 459076

T.I.C. Inverness,
Castle Wynd Tel 01463 234353

Walking Times

In giving approximate times, I have taken account of heights climbed and terrain encountered.

		Hours	Min
Fort William	**to Gairlochy**	**3**	**30**
Gairlochy	**to Fort Augustus**	**9**	**45**
Fort Augustus	**to Invermoriston**	**3**	**45**
Invermoriston	**to Drumnadrochit**	**6**	**30**
Drumnadrochit to Inverness		**8**	**00**
		31	**30**

Distances

Day			Miles	Km
1	**Fort William**	**to Gairlochy**	**10.5**	**16.8**
2	**Gairlochy**	**to Fort Augustus**	**22.5**	**36**
3	**Fort Augustus**	**to Invermoriston**	**8**	**12.8**
4	**Invermoriston**	**to Drumnadrochit**	**14**	**22.4**
5	**Drumnadrochit to Inverness**		**18**	**28.8**
			73	**116.**

Grid References

This section has been included to assist walkers, particularly those who have a G.P.S. system, to locate precise positions on route. You may also find it helpful to use in conjunction with the relevant O.S. map of the area.

Starting Plinth in Fort William	G.R. 104743
Path near Playing Fields	G.R. 100765
Towpath before Neptune's Staircase	G.R. 108765
Neptune's Staircase	G.R. 115771
Towpath to Gairlochy	G.R. 145808
Road out of Gairlochy	G.R. 176844
Beginning of Loch Lochy	G.R. 188856
Forest at Clunes	G.R. 211890
South Laggan Forest	G.R. 256936
Great Glen Water Park	G.R. 302982
Forest Track Loch Oich	G.R. 328015
Canal at Cullochy	G.R. 341044
Minor Road out of Fort Augustus	G.R. 379100
Forest Track near Portclair	G.R. 415140
Forest Track above Invermoriston	G.R. 425170
Temple House, Tychat	G.R. 534302
Ladycairn	G.R. 556383
Finishing Plinth in Inverness	G.R. 667452

Glossary of Words

Burn - *Scottish word meaning stream, brook, beck or watercourse.*

Glen - *Scottish word for a valley.*

Grid Reference - *Derived from the national grid reference system. This is used to pinpoint a place on a map by use of letters and numbers.*

Gully - *A narrow channel or cleft in a rock face, may have waterfalls and can be very slippery and have vertical drops.*

Kissing Gate - *Swing gate that usually lets one person through it at a time by moving the gate backwards and forwards.*

Loch - *Scottish word for lake.*

Lock – *Not to be confused with above. Means canal water lock.*

Metalled Road - *Generally known as a stone chipping road. This term evolved and became regarded as the roads metal or the roads surface.*

Outcrop - *Part of a rock formation that sticks out from the main body of rock.*

Route Card - *A plan of action prepared before you leave. A copy to be left with someone so that if you fail to return by a planned time then help can be summoned.*

Summit - *The highest point of a mountain or hill.*

Trig Point - *True name is Triangulation Pillar. These mark the summit of many mountains but not all. It is a small stone pillar with a number on it. The height of the mountain is taken from this point.*

Useful Addresses/Tel No's

Long Distance Walkers Association (L.D.W.A.)
Brian Smith
10 Temple Park Close
Leeds L.S.15 0JJ
Tel. 0113 2642205
This association is set up to further the interests of those who enjoy long distance walking. Members receive a journal three times each year, which includes information on all aspects of long distance walking.

Ramblers Association
2nd Floor, Camelford House,
87-90 Albert Embankment,
London SE1 7TW
Tel. 01577 861222
Local groups with regular meetings.

The Great Glen Way Ranger Service,
Auchterawe,
Fort Augustus, PH32 4BT
Tel. 01320 366633
www.greatglenway.com

Citylink. Tel. 08705 505050. Information on bus times between Fort William and Inverness.

Easyjet. Tel. 0870 6000000
British Airways. Tel. 08457 733377
Inverness Airport. Tel01667 464000

National Rail Services. Tel. 08457 484950
Scotrail Ticket Purchases. Tel. 08457 550033

Clansman Taxis, Fort William. Tel: 01397 703334

Aberchalder Baggage Transfer Service, 01809 501411 for walkers and cyclists. Transport your baggage from Fort William to Inverness and all points in between.

Hopefully you have enjoyed this walk and gained as much pleasure from walking the route as I did. Should you wish to walk another route, please visit Challenge Publications website at: -

www.chall-pub.fsnet.co.uk

A wide selection of walking guides covering the UK is available including 'The National Three Peaks Walk'. The top selling and main book covering the famous three peaks routes and containing everything you need to know to complete the challenge.

On our website you will find other interesting, and possibly different walks around the British Isles, which are equally as picturesque and enjoyable as this one.

Should you wish to comment on this book or give further information to help keep the book updated then please write to the address below or e mail via the website. An acknowledgement will be given: -

Challenge Publications
7, Earlsmere Drive,
Ardsley
Barnsley
S71 5HH

OTHER SCOTTISH BOOKS AVAILABLE FROM CHALLENGE PUBLICATIONS:-

NATIONAL 3 PEAKS WALK:
The top selling book with sketch maps, colour photos, B&B's and driving route between the 3 peaks of Ben Nevis, Scafell Pike and Snowdon. Full route description included.
ISBN 0-9526900-7-1   £6.50

THE SCOTTISH COAST TO COAST WALK:
A classic route from Oban to St. Andrews with full description, campsites, B&B's & photos etc.
ISBN 0-9526900-8-X   £6.50

JOHN O GROATS TO LANDS END:
Go for the big one. The shortest route by road. See how to do it and how to avoid the blisters! Extensive information on all aspects from fund raising to the preparation and walk.
ISBN 0-9526900-4-7   £7.50

View them on our website, see page 54 for details on how to order direct, post free.

NOTES

NOTES